ON THE SPOT

NO PREP GAMES
FOR YOUTH MINISTRY

Group

LOVELAND, CO

www.group.com

CONTENTS

ON THE SPOT: NO-PREP GAMES FOR YOUTH MINISTRY

Copyright © 2008 Group Publishing, Inc.
Visit our website: **group.com**

All rights reserved. No part of this book may be reproduced in any manner whatsoever without prior written permission from the publisher, except where noted in the text and in the case of brief quotations embodied in critical articles and reviews. For information, e-mail Permissions at inforights@group.com, or write Permissions, Group Publishing, Inc., P.O. Box 481, Loveland, CO 80539.

CREDITS

Editor: Steve Parolini
Project Manager: Pam Clifford
Executive Developer: Amy Nappa
Chief Creative Officer: Joani Schultz
Art Director: Jeff Storm

Cover and Interior
Designer: Nathan Crutchfield
Production Manager: Peggy Naylor

Unless otherwise indicated, all Scripture quotations are taken from the *Holy Bible*, New Living Translation, copyright © 1996, 2004. Used by permission of Tyndale House Publishers, Inc., Carol Stream, Illinois 60188. All rights reserved.

ISBN 978-0-7644-3676-5
10 9 8 7
17 16 15 14 13 12 11 10
Printed in the United States of America.

Introduction

The phrase "on the spot" usually has negative connotations. Ever been put on the spot at work? Perhaps you've been called upon to offer an impromptu speech in front of a group of unsympathetic peers. Nothing brings on the flop sweat like being put on the spot.

Well, we're turning that phrase upside down. Now "on the spot" is all about fun, not fear. It's all about possibility, not panic. Are things dragging in your youth group meeting? You can fix that on the spot. Just choose a game from these pages and liven things up in an instant. Find yourself with a moment between activities, surrounded by a crowd of restless teenagers? Flip to a game in this book and turn that boredom into fun.

On the Spot games are easy to lead and require no props (except for the occasional chair or items group members already have in their possession). In fact, these are so easy to use, you don't have to plan ahead at all. (Thus, the whole "on the spot" theme we've been promoting.) The games in this book work well as crowdbreakers or time-eaters or just-for-fun-ers. You'll be cheered as a hero for saving the day. Revered for your ability to "think on your feet." (Okay, maybe "read on your feet" is more accurate. But it's still a valuable skill worthy of reverence.) Or maybe you'll just end up turning a down time into an up one.

Forget the flop sweat. Have fun with your group instead. Right where you are. Right now.

On the spot.

1 | I Never...

This is a high-energy game, full of action and laughter, that will keep everyone on their toes.

In this mixer, you'll need to make sure there is one chair for each person and that there's plenty of room for moving around. Form a circle with the chairs, with one in the middle. Every person takes a chair, with one being in the center chair, or the "mush pot." The person in the mush pot begins by completing the sentence, "I have never..." with something he or she has never done, but something that someone else in the circle might have done. So for example, the person in the mush pot might say, "I have never been skydiving," or "I have never been to Australia."

As soon as the first person makes his or her statement, everyone in the circle who has had that experience must get up and find a new chair as quickly as possible. The last person standing has to take the chair in the mush pot. It's possible that no one will get up, in which case, the person in the middle takes another turn. Try to continue until everyone has had a chance to be in the mush pot.

The object of the game is to get to know interesting things about each other, and have a lot of fun doing it.

2 If You...

This game is a twist on the previous game, I Never.

Have everyone sit in a circle. You'll have one less chair than you have players, and the player without a chair must stand in the middle of the circle. Explain that you're going to read a series of statements that all begin with "If you..." When you say "go," everyone who has done what the statement describes must find a new place to sit, leaving a new person in the middle. This is one of those games that really doesn't have a winner, so you can play for as long as you have statements or questions. To add to the fun, include a few statements that you're sure to include everyone, so the entire circle must get up and move.

Here are a few to get you started:
• *If you have ever fallen asleep in church...*
• *If you have ever broken a bone...*
• *If you have ever spilled something in a restaurant...*
• *If you have ever slipped and fallen in a public place...*
• *If you have ever put your shoes on the wrong feet...*
• *If you like sausage on your pizza...*
• *If you know Psalm 23 by heart...*
• *If you have ever had a "bad hair day"...*
• *If you can remember your first grade teacher's name...*
• *If you talk to plants...*

Players must follow instructions to form groups as quickly as they can. Explain that you will be calling out categories, and in 20 seconds or less everyone must join with others who fit the same description.

To begin, have the whole group mill around, mixing randomly until you call out a category. After you call out a category, allow 20 seconds and call time. Then stop and see how people grouped themselves. Have everyone mill around the room again until you call a new category. Continue as time allows.

Use the following categories, or make up your own:
- *same hair color*
- *same birthday month*
- *same color shoes*
- *had the same thing for breakfast*
- *same color eyes*
- *same favorite food*
- *watched the same show on TV last night*
- *same favorite drink*
- *same favorite class subject*
- *live in the same color building or house*
- *same favorite ice cream flavor*

Option: You can also play this as an elimination game. Those who don't find at least one partner each round have to sit down until there are just one or two players left.

4 Third Person

This is a simple activity you can use to make getting to know you interesting!

Gather everyone in a circle for this Q-and-A crowdbreaker—the catch is that each person has to answer questions in the third person (meaning they refer to themselves by name instead of using "I").

Use fun questions such as:
- Tell a story about a time when you met someone famous.
- Describe your ultimate summer vacation.
- Talk about the earliest memory you have.
- Explain how you would prepare for a job interview with Steven Spielberg or Bill Gates.
- Describe your Saturday morning routine.
- Talk about the strangest thing that's ever happened to you.
- Tell about a meal you like to prepare for yourself and how it's done.

5 When I Was a Kid

Form two teams of equal number. Tell teams that each person should come up with a memorable story from childhood. The events can be funny, embarrassing, serious, or outlandish.

Give teams several minutes to meet and tell their stories. If possible, teams should meet away from each other, so they can't overhear each other's stories. Each team should then choose which stories they are going to share with the whole group. Teams should also decide who is going to relate which stories. The person telling the story can be the person who actually experienced it, or it can be someone who tries to convince the other team the incident actually happened to him or her.

When everyone is ready, call teams together, and have them take turns telling stories. After someone tells a story, invite the other team to guess who really experienced the incident. Give teams one point for every correct guess and one point for every time the other team guesses wrong. The team with the most points at the end wins.

Encourage everyone to really ham it up when they tell the stories.

Middle Name Intros

Give everyone a minute or two to come up with an original middle name. This can be a one-word name, a multiple-word name, or a famous person's name, but it must describe something about them. For example, "Sparkles-a-lot" could describe someone who enjoys fine jewelry. "Climber" could identify someone who enjoys rock climbing, "Tiger Woods" a golf fanatic, or "Mozart" someone who enjoys classical music.

Go around the circle and have everyone introduce themselves, explaining their new middle names.

My Favorite Things

Have everyone stand in the middle of the room. Explain that you are going to read a list of categories. Each time you name a category, group members must call out their favorite thing in that category. Have them continue calling it out until they find other people who have the same favorite. For example, if you call out "movie," everyone will begin calling out the title of his or her favorite movie. Those who call out the name of the same movie are to form a group. Inevitably there will be people who will be the only one with a favorite thing. That's okay. It's a good reminder of how diverse your group is, and the unique interests of all group members.

Here are some suggestions for categories you may wish to call out:

- *pizza topping*
- *dessert*
- *singer or band*
- *color*
- *movie*
- *sport*
- *season*
- *holiday*

Meet in the Middle

8

Form a circle. Explain that when you call out a phrase that describes anyone in the group, the people it describes are to walk to the middle of the circle and introduce themselves to everyone else who comes into the middle. Start by naming items of clothing, such as jeans or sneakers, and then move to hobbies or favorite foods. You can also use phrases such as "one sibling," "loves sports," or "book lover."

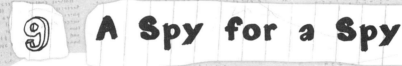

9 A Spy for a Spy

Before you begin, secretly choose three group members to be spies. Give them code names, such as "Pink Panther," "007," or "Maxwell Smart."

Instruct participants that their mission is to find the three spies. They'll have several minutes to mingle. Group members must each approach a person, shake hands, and ask his or her name. Then, while still holding hands, they must ask if this person is either the Pink Panther, 007, or Maxwell Smart. (Note: they may ask only one code name at a time.) A "no" response is one squeeze of the hand; a "yes" response is two squeezes of the hand.

When group members find a spy, they aren't to reveal the spy's identity, but continue meeting others. When a person thinks he or she has discovered the true identity of all three spies, this person must report to "headquarters" (the leader) and reveal the spies' names. The first person to learn all three spies' real names wins.

10   The Shoe Pile

Have participants walk around the room, talking to each other and finding out as much about others as they can. Suggest that they ask about each other's favorites—vacation spots, authors, or movies, for example. After about five minutes, call everyone together, and ask each person to put one shoe into a pile. Then have everyone sit in a circle and try to hide his or her other shoe by sitting on that foot (so others can't use it as a clue to figure out who the missing shoe belongs to). Have one person at a time go to the shoe pile, select a shoe that belongs to someone else, try to match it to its owner, and then tell what he or she learned about that person. You can ask other group members to contribute facts they learned about that person, as well.

11   Human Tic-Tac-Toe

You'll need to set up nine chairs in three rows, just like the sections on a tic-tac-toe diagram. Then divide your group into two teams. Each team takes its turn by sending one person to sit in a selected chair. The first team to get three in a row wins. Beware, since you're not using X's and O's, this can get confusing and laughter will ensue!

To make it a bit more exciting, establish a time limit that each team member has to select a seat. For example, you might allow five seconds after the last group member sat down for the next to reach the chosen chair.

12 Wacky Questions

Have everyone stand or sit in a circle. One at a time, have each one state his or her name and give a response to one of the wacky questions below, which may or may not be related to your meeting topic.

The possibilities for questions are endless, but here's a sample of some questions you might ask:
- *What's your favorite product with milk in it?*
- *What's your favorite underarm deodorant, and which pit do you hit first?*
- *What's your favorite chore around the house?*
- *What's the grossest food you've ever eaten?*
- *What's the worst movie you've ever seen?*
- *What's the strangest nonsense sound you can think of?*

13 Zip, Zoom, Zowie

Form two teams of equal number. Have them form two single-file lines on one side of the room, and place a chair or some other object at the opposite side.

This is a relay of creativity. Group members will each select their own way of getting to the chair and back, but each one must move in a way that hasn't been used before. They can hop on one foot, hop on two feet, run, walk backward, skip, walk heel to toe, somersault, or use any other movement as long as no one else has done it before.

To add a sense of urgency, time the race. Then hold a second relay to see if teams can improve on their first time. During the second round, tell group members that they can do the relay any way they want, whether someone has done it before or not.

14 Quick Sort

Form two teams. Explain that you are going to call out categories, and each team will need to sort itself as quickly as possible into a line in the order you have suggested. For example, if you say, "Sort by age, youngest to oldest," teams should form a line with the youngest person on one end and the oldest person at the other.

Before keeping score, it would be a good idea to have several practice rounds. Then award a point each round to the team that gets in line most quickly. Some categories might call for rough estimates, but team members should be able to defend their individual positions and the order in which they've arranged themselves.

Here are some sorting suggestions to get you started:
- *Sort by height from shortest to tallest.*
- *Sort by shoe size from largest to smallest.*
- *Sort by the number of states you have visited, most states to fewest.*
- *Sort by the farthest distance ever traveled, from farthest distance to shortest distance.*
- *Sort by the number of instruments you play, most to least.*
- *Sort by the number of times you've moved, least to most.*
- *Sort by the number of siblings you have, least to most.*
- *Sort by the number of sodas you drink in a day, most to least.*
- *Sort by the number of trees in your yard, most to least.*
- *Sort by the number of movies you've been to this year, least to most.*
- *Sort by the number of traffic violations you've had, most to least.*

15 Sound Bite

In this game, each player thinks of a famous person and a three-word quote that will help identify that person. The quote can be either a real statement from history or an imaginary quote that acts as a clue to the person's identity. For example, the person could be a historical personality (Lincoln: "Four-score and seven…"), a movie character (Arnold Schwarzenegger: "I'll be back!"), or a Bible character (Noah: "On the boat!").

Have players take turns giving clues as the other group members try to guess each character's identity.

As a fun variation, have group members identify their famous person by using three words that suggest the person's identity, rather than using quotes. For example, Abraham Lincoln might be described with the three words Gettysburg, tall, and president.

16 Working Together

Use this game as a time filler or as a way to get group members interacting with one another. Have participants get into pairs, and then explain that they must create a "secret handshake." It can contain as many different moves and actions as they like; for example, high-fives, knocking elbows, twirling in a circle, and snapping their fingers. Encourage them to be as creative as possible. After each pair has had some time to create, have them demonstrate their handshakes. Offer "virtual prizes" (nothing more than the idea of a prize) for the handshakes voted craziest, most creative, and most time-consuming.

17 Top Ten Lists

Hold up any object in the room or on your person, such as a coin, a shoe, or a ring, and ask group members to think of ten things they could do with the object.

For instance, a coin can be a marker on a board game, worn on your nose in a relay, flipped to decide who goes first, rolled on its edge, and so on. Encourage creativity!

Continue holding up objects you can find in the room, and see what creative ideas everyone can come up with.

If you give each round a time limit, you can turn it into a competition by having teams compete to come up with as many reasonable uses as possible during that time limit. Award a point for each "approved" idea. The team with the most points at the end of the rounds wins. For their prize, have them come up with as many ways of saying "Thank you!" as possible in the same time limit.

18 Gimme Five!

Form groups of three, and explain that the object of this game is for groups to try to name five items in a category that you will call out. When members of a trio can name five items, they need to jump up and yell, *"Gimme five!"* Then trio members must share the items they came up with so the rest of the group can verify them. When a trio presents five verified items in the category, that trio wins the category.

19 Who Am I?

This is a game that not only challenges group members' knowledge of Bible characters, but will turn them on to Bible facts and discovering the truth.

Choose a volunteer to go first. Have him or her pick a Bible character and tell the other participants three things about this character without revealing the character's name. The catch is that only two of the three statements can be true. One of the three must be false.

For example, if the group member is thinking of Paul, he or she might say:
• *This person wrote some of the Bible (true).*
• *This person was one of the 12 disciples (false).*
• *This person could not walk on water (true—he almost drowned when he was shipwrecked).*

Each player may then ask the volunteer one question that can be answered with a "yes" or "no." Then all the players are to vote on which statement was not true.

After the vote, the volunteer reveals which statement was false, and the other players can take turns guessing who the Bible character really is.

Play until each group member who wants to has had a turn.

20 Count 'Em

Form teams and have them tally points according to team members' answers to these statements:

- *Add your team members' ages.*
- *Give 20 points for each person whose birthday is in December or January.*
- *Give 5 points for each person who made his or her bed this morning.*
- *Give 1 point for each brother or sister team members have.*
- *Give 1 point for each book of the Bible your team can name.*
- *Give 10 points for each person whose first name can be found in the Bible.*

After teams tally their points, have them divide the total by the number of people in their team. Then see if each person on the team can think of that same number of gifts God has given to him or her.

21 Laws and Guffaws

In this game, group members must discover what unwritten law is governing the game.

Choose two or three people to stand outside hearing distance of the rest of the group. Have the rest of the group then decide on a "law" they're going to observe in answering any question they may be asked. For example, they may decide that group members must pull on their ears before answering, begin each answer with the word "the", or cover their mouths with their hands after each answer. They may be as creative as they want in establishing the law, but they must come to an agreement within two minutes.

Have the "outsiders" return and begin asking group members questions. The outsiders can confer about what they notice in the answers. Play until the outsiders either figure out the law or give up, and then let them each choose a person as a replacement and play another round.

22 What If...

This game works best with groups that have been together for a while.

Form a circle, and have one person be "It." Ask that person to leave the room. While he or she is out of the room, have the remaining group members decide which of them will be the mystery person.

When "It" returns, have him or her ask questions about the mystery person, such as *"What if this person were a color? What color would he or she be?"* or *"What if this person were a shoe? What kind of shoe would he or she be?"* After each question, group members must choose an answer with characteristics similar to the mystery person. For example, if the mystery person is cheerful, he or she might be the color yellow. Or if the mystery person is athletic, he or she might be a Nike tennis shoe.

Have group members answer the questions, and then have "It" guess who the mystery person is. Whether the guess is right or wrong, have the mystery person reveal him- or herself. This person is "It" for the next round of play. Some other possible objects for the question *"What if this person were a...?"* could include animal, automobile, body of water, boat, chair, household appliance, flower, piece of clothing, kind of music, type of house, vegetable, tool, means of transportation, or kind of art.

23 Take Your Pick

This can easily be played in pairs, trios, or larger groups, depending on your number of participants. In this game, group members take turns asking each other questions that require the person answering to make a choice.

For example, group members might have to decide between:
- *ice cream or pizza*
- *the beach or Disneyland*
- *reading a book or playing a video game*
- *swimming laps or lying in the sun*
- *cats or dogs*
- *getting up early or late*

You can turn this game into a discussion of faith and moral issues by asking other types of questions. For example, group members might have to decide between gossiping or keeping someone's confidence.

Be sure everyone is allowed the opportunity to explain why he or she chose one thing over another. After you've provided a few questions, take turns letting group members think up items, destinations, or activities for others to choose between.

24 All For One

Form groups of four. In this game, all four group members must agree on one thing. For example, you might ask what snack food they enjoy. Each group must find an answer everyone agrees on. If even one person doesn't agree, they must find another answer. This isn't as easy as it sounds!

Read each of the following phrases aloud, and allow time for each group to agree upon an answer:

- something you like to do when you have free time
- a snack food you like to eat
- a story of Jesus you like
- a place you like to go for fun
- a holiday you enjoy
- a TV program you enjoy

25 The Master Potter

Select one person who will serve as your model. Have the other participants form pairs. One member of each pair will be the "clay" while the other will be the "artist." Explain that the model is going to pose for all the artists, and it's their job to re-create the model's pose with their clay.

Give the model a couple of minutes to choose a character from the Bible, and to think of a pose that represents a significant event in that person's life. For example, the model might choose Saul being struck by a bright light, or Simon of Cyrene carrying Christ's cross.

When you give the signal, all those who are clay must close their eyes and keep them closed while the model strikes and holds the pose. Only the artists are allowed to see the model. Then it is their job to give verbal directions to their clay, molding them with words only. They may not touch their partner.

Give partners a few minutes to work. Before allowing the clay people to open their eyes, have the model end the pose. Only the clay people should stay in position.

Once everyone has had a look around at all the different sculptures, have them guess what Bible character or event was being re-created.

26 Skit Tag

Form five or six small groups. Call the first group into a different room while the rest of the groups do something else. Instruct the first group to make up a short, two- to three-minute silent skit based on a given Bible passage.

When they're ready, have this group return and perform the skit in front of everyone. Make sure the second group knows to pay close attention—they'll need to get up and repeat that skit immediately! Have the second group perform the skit from memory, in front of everyone, with third group repeating the skit from memory right after that.

Continue until all the groups have done their version of the skit. By the time the last group performs, the skit is usually hilariously different. Have the last group perform the skit for the entire group, and then have the first group perform the original skit again.

27 Hall of Fame

Pick a volunteer to begin building a "Hall of Fame" by pantomiming (no speaking aloud) a famous person or musician of his or her choice. All other group members are to try and guess who the person is. Whoever guesses correctly gets to pantomime next.

After performing a pantomime, a player can't guess for the remainder of the game and is considered a part of the Hall of Fame. That doesn't mean the fun is over. Whenever another player begins to pantomime, all previous pantomimers should sing or talk like their famous person, creating quite a distraction and inviting plenty of laughter.

The excitement builds until there is only one player left. This person must quiet the group by calling out each famous person individually. Once called, the person nods off to faux sleep (no snoring!), and the final person can complete his or her pantomime.

28 Hello-Goodbye

Gather everyone together and tell them you're going to play the Hello-Goodbye game. Do your best Queen Elizabeth imitation and wave "royally" at various people in the group, saying, "Hello. Goodbye."

After you've waved to several people, ask, "*Who did I wave to?*" Group members will respond by naming one of the people at whom you aimed your wave. But the trick of the game is this: The first person to speak or make a noise after you ask, "*Who did I wave to?*" is the person you actually "waved to." So, for example, if you aimed your wave at Sarah, then asked, "*Who did I wave to?*" and Jim says, "*Sarah,*" you'd say, "*No, I waved at you.*" Or if Joshua had sneezed just before Jim spoke, you'd say, "*No, I waved at Joshua.*" Give a treat, such as a Hershey's Kiss, to the first person to correctly guess whom you "waved to."

Don't give an explanation about the method to your madness; just repeat the game until someone catches on. When a group member finally does figure out the pattern, tell him or her not to explain it to the group. Instead, have that person attempt to lead the Hello-Goodbye game. That way you'll know whether the person has actually figured it out or not. Play until everyone has figured out the game.

29 Charade Twists

In a pinch? Love charades? Try any one of these variations to keep things hopping:

• Go for It
In this moving version of Charades, a group member can either stay put and act out a word or run to find something in the church (or meeting place) to help act it out. For soap opera, for example, she can run to a bathroom, grab some soap, then pretend to sing dramatically.

• Stumpers
Each team thinks of words for the opposite team to act out, and the goal is to stump the other team. To make things even more interesting, limit some rounds to just nouns or verbs. Some favorite stumpers include oysters and appendage.

• What Am I?
Team members must act out nouns by becoming them. Start with easy words, such as dog and cheerleader, then move to harder words, such as dinosaur and candle.

• Sound Effects
Players can make as much noise as they want to act out words such as garbage disposal. For more laughs, combine Sound Effects Charades with another version.